Ann Gianola

The Stolen Pharaoh

DELTA Publishing

You can listen to *The Stolen Pharaoh* using the free DELTA Augmented app – you'll also find fun interactive activities!

Download the free DELTA Augmented app onto your device	Start picture recognition and scan the **contents page**	Download files and use them now or save them for later

1st edition   1 ⁵ ⁴ ³ ² ¹ | 2026 25 24 23 22

Delta Publishing, 2022
www.deltapublishing.co.uk

© Ernst Klett Sprachen GmbH, Rotebühlstraße 77, 70178 Stuttgart, 2022

Author Text: Ann Gianola
Annotations and activities: Bernardo Morales
Editor: Kate Baade

Cover and layout: Andreas Drabarek, Eva Lettenmayer
Illustrations: Dusan Lakicevic, Beehive Illustration
Design: Datagroup int, Timisoara
Cover picture: Dusan Lakicevic, Beehive Illustration
Printing and binding: Plump Druck & Medien GmbH, Rheinbreitbach

Printed in Germany
ISBN 978-3-12-501160-1

Contents

Abbreviations

sb   somebody
sth   something

Photos:
5 123RF.com (matriyoshka), Nidderau; **5** 123RF.com (macrovector), Nidderau;
81 123RF.com (martialred), Nidderau; **82** 123RF.com (Taras Dubov), Nidderau;
82 123RF.com (teravector), Nidderau

Before you start

1. Ancient Egypt
What do you know about Ancient Egypt? Write some words in the box below.

2. Art theft
This story is based on the theft of a precious Egyptian work of art. More than 50,000 works of art are stolen around the world each year. The black market for stolen art is valued between $6-8 billion each year.

Do some research. Find out:
- why art theft is so popular.
- what happens to stolen works of art.
- how the money used to trade stolen art is spent.
- how museums handle security.

3. Repatriation
Many paintings, artifacts and sculptures displayed in western museums were originally stolen. There is increasing pressure to return, or repatriate, works of art to their country of origin. Museums around the world, such as the Smithsonian's National Museum of African Art, have started taking stolen works of

art off display. Their director, Ngaire Blankenberg, says that displaying looted artworks does "a huge amount of harm".

Brainstorm arguments from the two points of view below.

Reasons to continue displaying stolen works of art	Reasons to repatriate stolen works of art

4. The story
Read the story. Which character do you like best? What did you discover about the world of art theft?

Chapter 1

Sanjay took a deep breath. Then he let it out slowly. He sat
nervously across from Detective Jacobs at the police station,
answering her questions over and over again. Yet, the Egyptian
pharaoh was still missing. And, unfortunately, the sixteen-year-
old was one of the last people to see it. Although he observed the
head only briefly, he could remember its face–almond-shaped
eyes, full lips, and serene expression–sculpted in stone. How
incredible that it was over three thousand years old. The next
thing he knew, the lights went out and the museum was in total
darkness. By the time the lights came back on, the artifact, valued
at over five million dollars, had disappeared.

Sanjay was a student volunteer, working at the Westbrook
Museum for a few hours a week. But he was there that night–

---

19 **to take a deep breath** to breathe deeply before you do sth that makes you nervous –
22 **pharaoh** a ruler in ancient Egypt – 24 **briefly** for a short time – 25 **to sculpt** to make
out of stone – 28 **artifact** sth made in the past that is historically important

after hours–preparing for the opening of the exhibit the next day. Sanjay was with a handful of others: Mrs. Harwood, the museum's executive director; Charlotte, the curator; Amir, the security officer; Silvia, the cashier in the gift shop; Pierre the tour guide; and Felix, the custodian.

Moments before the blackout, Felix had given Sanjay some directions. "Let's clean the glass before we lock it up," he said, pointing to a soft cloth and a spray bottle. "The public needs a crystal-clear view of this one." Indeed, displaying the ancient artwork was a major event for the small museum. The Westbrook definitely wasn't the Louvre. It was an ordinary two-story building with a very limited collection. A 1950s pencil sketch by Picasso, worth only a few thousand dollars, was considered its most valuable asset.

Showcasing an Egyptian sculpture from the 1300s BCE was a dream come true. Amazingly, Mrs. Harwood had arranged the deal with a private collector, proving that she had some surprising connections in the art world. The piece was on loan for exactly one month–and promised to attract visitors from around the globe. It would also be a gift to the community: a rare glimpse of antiquity and a huge moneymaker for the local businesses.

Sadly, the Westbrook Museum was now famous in a bad way. The pharaoh was mysteriously stolen within reach of seven individuals, including Sanjay. And Detective Jacobs thought that at least one of them was guilty. "Are you trying to tell me," she asked, drumming her fingers on her desk, "that something worth five *million* dollars was left unguarded...out in the open?"

"Um, yes," answered Sanjay, running a hand through his thick black hair. "We were just setting up. It wasn't locked in its glass case yet, and the alarms weren't activated."

---

2 **handful** a small amount – 6 **blackout** when there is no light due to an electrical power failure – 9 **crystal-clear** extremely clear – 9 **to display** to show – 9 **ancient** from a very long time ago – 18 **on loan** *(here)* in a different place for a limited amount of time – 20 **glimpse** see sth for a limited time – 21 **moneymaker** sth used to make money – 25 **guilty** responsible for having committed a crime

"When the electricity failed," stated the detective, shaking her head, "there was a backup generator to provide another power source. And, at very least, didn't anyone have a flashlight or a cell phone...to see what was happening?"

"You might think so," said Sanjay, squirming in his chair. "Except the backup generator was broken, apparently. Then no one seemed to have a flashlight–and we're not supposed to carry cell phones around the museum."

"So, you want me to believe that a person picked up a priceless artifact during a suspicious power outage...and hid it somewhere?"

"I know it sounds ridiculous," replied Sanjay. He took another deep breath and let it out slowly. "But, to my knowledge, that's exactly what happened."

> What disappeared from the museum?

> How old was the artifact?

Think about it... ?

> Why do you think it is difficult for small museums to attract visitors?

> How was it possible for someone to steal the pharaoh?

2 **backup** sth that is used in case sth stops working – 3 **flashlight** a small portable light usually powered by batteries – 5 **to squirm** to move nervously from side to side – 9 **priceless** too valuable to have a price – 10 **outage** a period of time when a service is interrupted

Chapter 2

The **theft** at the Westbrook Museum was international news. Mrs. Harwood was, of course, horrified by the negative publicity. Outside the museum, a **crowd** of reporters bombarded her with questions: "Where is the pharaoh hidden?" asked one. "Sounds like it was an inside job," observed another. "Any idea who did it? And what does this mean for you–and the future of the Westbrook?" **inquired** a third, **nodding** toward the police tape around the building.

Accompanied by Detective Jacobs, Mrs. Harwood kept her head down and ignored them. "They have no respect," she **grumbled**, tightening her fists. "I've been a leader in this town for fifty years," she continued, "trying to bring art and culture to *the people*. And this is the thanks I get! Next, they'll be accusing *me* of stealing the pharaoh."

19 **theft** the act of taking sth that belongs to sb else – 21 **crowd** a large group of people – 24 **to inquire** to ask – 25 **to nod** to move your head up and down – 28 **to grumble** to say sth in an angry way

"It's a big story, Mrs. Harwood," said Detective Jacobs, sweeping her dark curly hair away from her eyes. "An object worth five million dollars disappeared in an instant. I'm afraid you'll have to get used to the attention for a while–until we find out where it is."

Mrs. Harwood clucked her tongue with annoyance. For the past three hours, she had taken the detective and two other police officers through the museum, once again examining every inch of it. And the whole business exhausted her. Detective Jacobs was patient with Mrs. Harwood–after all, she was seventy-six years old. Still, she was there on the night of the robbery, and therefore remained a suspect. The idea, however, infuriated the executive director. "Like I've told you–and the FBI (Federal Bureau of Investigation)–I'm the richest woman around," she declared proudly, her arms open wide. "I don't need to steal art treasures from Egypt...or anywhere else."

Instead, Mrs. Harwood pointed the finger elsewhere. "Let me tell you about Sanjay," she began. "He's a nice boy, but sometimes school kids do silly pranks. You should talk to him again." Next, she mentioned Charlotte: "Our curator is a capable employee. But she's an opportunist. I'm sure she wants to climb the ladder in the art world. Speak to her too, obviously." Later, she referred to Amir: "He's our *security* person–but has Egyptian ancestry, I think. Maybe he wanted to take the pharaoh home. And Felix, the custodian, certainly knew his way around the Westbrook." Mrs. Harwood rubbed her chin thoughtfully. "All of their salaries are modest," she added. "Poor Silvia, the cashier in the gift shop, and Pierre, our tour guide. I don't know how they keep food on their tables. Five million dollars would be quite tempting, I imagine."

Finally, they arrived at Mrs. Harwood's car. As her chauffeur opened the passenger door, she turned to the detective. "The

---

5 **to cluck your tongue** to make a sound with your tongue to show you are not happy – 11 **suspect** sb who the police think has committed a crime – 11 **to infuriate** to make angry – 16 **to point the finger elsewhere** to accuse sb else – 18 **prank** a trick that is supposed to be funny but not meant to hurt anyone – 24 **custodian** sb who takes care of things in a building – 25 **chin** the lower, pointy part of your face – 29 **chauffeur** driver

museum staff is lovely, really. It's unbearable to think that any one of them would commit such a dreadful crime. Someone was desperate, I suppose. It's tragic."

"Human beings sometimes make bad decisions," noted Detective Jacobs. "And the pharaoh is worth a fortune."

"But they can't sell it," Mrs. Harwood stated firmly. "It's stolen. No museum in the world will touch it. Neither will a legitimate auction house. The story is everywhere. Anyway, I've really told you all that I can. Sorry I can't be more helpful to you."

"I appreciate your time," said Detective Jacobs. Then she watched as Mrs. Harwood's chauffeur drove out of the parking lot and around the corner. "And you've actually been very helpful," the detective whispered to herself. "I'm sure we'll talk again soon."

> Why did Mrs. Harwood think Sanjay could have taken the pharaoh?

> Why does Mrs. Harwood think the thief won't be able to sell the pharaoh?

Think about it...

> Why do you think a museum staff member might want to steal the pharaoh?

> Why do you think somebody would want to steal an artifact like the pharaoh?

1 **unbearable** very unpleasant – 2 **dreadful** horrible – 7 **legitimate** honest – 13 **to whisper** to say sth very quietly

Chapter 3

"Mrs. Harwood described you as a *capable employee* ...but an *opportunist*," said Detective Jacobs, straightening the collar on her faux-leather jacket. In response, Charlotte nearly spit out her chai tea. The detective handed her a clean paper napkin.

"Mrs. Harwood is *something else*," responded Charlotte, dabbing at her mouth. "A *capable employee*? Yes, I'm very capable," she agreed, her green eyes flashing slightly with annoyance. "I have a Master of Fine Arts degree from New York University. And I've spent an additional five years on internships and fieldwork, handling some of the most valuable pieces of art in the world."

"That's most impressive," said the detective, watching as Charlotte carefully took another sip from her cup. This time, she

---

20 **opportunist** sb who tries to take advantage of every situation – 21 **faux-leather** a material similar to leather made of non-animal products – 24 **to dab** to touch sth lightly and quickly – 25 **slightly** a little bit – 27 **internship** a job that gives sb work experience – 31 **sip** a small mouthful of liquid

managed to swallow all of it. "You sound more than qualified for your job."

"But how can I possibly be her definition of an *opportunist*?" laughed Charlotte, her stylish brown hair framing her pretty face. "To begin with, an *opportunist* wouldn't be working at the Westbrook," she added, setting down her cup firmly. "It's an embarrassment in the museum world–with a third-rate collection. Even their Picasso is mediocre," she claimed with authority. "A real opportunist would have found a way to stay in New York."

"Then why didn't you stay there?" asked the detective curiously.

"Because a person can't live in New York or any other major city on the pennies that most museum jobs pay," admitted Charlotte. "Two years ago, I decided that I could no longer survive on an insulting hourly wage. So, I moved here–into a large apartment with a view of an actual tree outside my window. Got a lot more for my money...and the job title of *curator*. However, I've mostly regretted it," she continued, sighing audibly. "I don't like living here. I honestly don't."

"Did acquiring the pharaoh–worth millions–influence your decision to remain in a job that you disliked and..."

"Detective," interrupted Charlotte, looking up from her cup. "I already gave a statement at the police station. And I was happy to meet with you–informally–here at the coffee shop. But I'm beginning to feel uncomfortable. Did I need the pharaoh to finance a penthouse on Park Avenue? Absolutely not!" she exclaimed firmly. "Working at the Westbrook hurt my career. And now, this theft will haunt me forever; I'll be judged as incompetent–and worse, unemployable. You must see that I am the complete opposite of an opportunist."

---

1 **to swallow** to make food and drink go down your throat into your stomach – 4 **stylish** fashionable – 8 **mediocre** not very good – 14 **wage** a set amount of money paid to an employee – 16 **curator** sb who is in charge of a museum – 17 **to sigh** *(here)* to breath loudly to show frustration – 25 **penthouse** an expensive apartment on the top floor of a building – 27 **to haunt** to cause problems for a long time – 28 **incompetent** not able to do a job well

"Still," persisted Detective Jacobs, "what happened at the Westbrook was a crime of *opportunity*–making the conditions perfect for *opportunists*–insiders–people who could take advantage of the situation and get what they wanted."

"Absolutely," said Charlotte, reaching for her purse. "Yet, it wasn't me. Was it Sanjay–because kids his age can do crazy things? Was it Silvia–so she could support her insane shopping habit?" Charlotte stood up. "Was it Pierre or Felix? Who knows? But, frankly, Mrs. Harwood was the real *opportunist* here. I mean, how was she–of all people on Earth–able to bring the pharaoh to the Westbrook?"

Detective Jacobs silently shared Charlotte's opinion. Any museum in the world would bend over backwards to display the ancient sculpture, handling it safely and securely. Yet, it magically appeared at the Westbrook... for a very short time...before vanishing.

Which degree did Charlotte have from New York University?

What does Charlotte think of the Picasso sketch at the Westbrook Museum?

Think about it...

What do you think someone like Charlotte would miss about New York? What do you think are the pros and cons of living in a big city?

Do you think Charlotte should be working at the Westbrook Museum?

3 **insider** sb who is part of a group and therefore has access to secrets – 7 **insane** crazy – 12 **to bend over backwards** to try very hard to achieve sth – 14 **to vanish** to disappear without leaving any trace

Chapter 4

Although Detective Jacobs worked in local law enforcement, she was also assisting a part of the FBI that focused on art crimes. Their goal was to recover high-value cultural property–the pharaoh, for example. Thefts of artwork happened frequently amounted to *billions* of dollars every year.

Someone at the Westbrook had a lot to gain by stealing the pharaoh. Mrs. Harwood, of course, was mistaken–or lied–that a stolen item was impossible to sell. Perhaps it couldn't be sold to modern museums or through legitimate auction houses. Yet, there were numerous buyers on the *black market*. And for many rich art collectors, it didn't matter how they got what they wanted. "There is a growing number of wealthy people," an FBI agent explained to Detective Jacobs, "and a shrinking

---

20 **goal** objective – 24 **to gain** to get sth that is in some way positive – 28 **black market** place where things are sold illegally – 30 **wealthy** rich – 30 **to shrink** to become smaller

number of precious things. Whether or not a sale is legal is often unimportant–and money is not an issue."

In the car, Detective Jacobs shook her head. "Imagine showing off the pharaoh to your friends...in the billiard room of your mansion," she thought. "Disgusting." Then, after checking an address on her phone, she parked in front of Amir's apartment building. She walked up a few steps and knocked on his door. Eventually, Amir, a good-looking man in his thirties, opened it.

"Hello, Detective," he said. "This is, um, unexpected."

"Yes," she replied. "Sorry I didn't call in advance. But I thought I might find you at home–you know, because the museum is closed." Amir shifted his feet uncomfortably in the entryway.

"Well, it's a mess in here, honestly," he said, blocking his doorway and hiding the detective's view of the inside. "Is it okay if we just talk here?"

"Sure," answered Detective Jacobs. "I'd like to clarify something, if you don't mind."

"I've already told you what I know," said Amir. "The Westbrook's security was appalling–inexcusable," he added, scratching at his dark, three-day beard. "Time and again, I begged Mrs. Harwood to increase our level of protection. We needed updated electronic systems and infrared motion detectors. We needed *armed* guards for this exhibit. But she was completely naïve. '*No one will steal anything, Amir*,' she claimed. '*This isn't the big city*.' She was so casual about it...like the pharaoh needed no more than a rusty bicycle lock.

"Very strange," agreed Detective Jacobs, noting Amir's frustration. "Today, however, my question is more personal: What do you think about the Egyptian artifacts spread all over the world? In your mind, is it ethical that so many are outside of Egypt?" Amir's face darkened with anger.

---

3 **to show off** to show sth you are proud of to other people – 10 **in advance** before a certain time – 14 **doorway** the space where the door opens and closes – 19 **appalling** very bad – 24 **naïve** believing sth that isn't true due to lack of life experience – 30 **ethical** morally correct

"No, it isn't!" he responded, suddenly speaking much louder. "Many of these treasures were *looted* from my country–well, uh, from the land of my ancestors. Then they were heartlessly sold to museums and collectors around the world."

"You're right," said Detective Jacobs, nodding her head.

"And these items are *sacred*," continued Amir passionately. "They were robbed from tombs and pyramids. Personally, I think it's a disgrace to capitalize on our brilliant ancient civilization." For a second, Amir threw up his hands in anger, letting the front door open slightly wider. Detective Jacobs quickly glanced past him into the living room. It was hardly a mess. In fact, it was empty, except for a few large boxes. To her, it looked like Amir was moving.

> In which two areas did Detective Jacobs work?

> Why does Amir think it is unethical for museums to display Egyptian artifacts?

Think about it ...

Why do you think Amir was blocking his doorway?

How far do you agree with Amir that African artifacts displayed in museums around the world be returned to their country of origin?

---

2 **looted** stolen during a violent event such as a riot – 3 **ancestor** sb who came from where you are from and who lived in a time before you – 6 **sacred** having an important religious meaning – 7 **tomb** a large structure where important people are buried – 10 **to glance** to take a quick look – 11 **hardly** almost not

---

Chapter 5

In the morning, Detective Jacobs was eating a piece of wheat
toast and reading her files. It was early in the investigation,
and she needed to gather more information. There had been
no searches of the suspects' homes. There had been no arrests.
But interestingly enough, the friendlier she was, the more the
Westbrook staff opened up to her. At least this was the case with
Mrs. Harwood, Charlotte, and Amir. The private chats were more
informative than the ones at the station.

On the surface, the people were likable. Sanjay, too, was a very
polite teenager. It was a shame that any one of them could be
guilty of art theft. Detective Jacobs didn't want anyone locked up
in prison. But there were serious consequences for this type of
crime. And her job, as a law enforcement officer, was finding the
pharaoh and holding the thief–or thieves–responsible.

At 1:00 p.m., the detective arrived at a shopping mall. She
went there to meet Silvia, the young woman who worked in the
Westbrook's gift shop. Silvia was standing in front of her favorite

18 **to gather** to collect – 26 **locked up** to be put in prison – 27 **consequence** result or
effect – 30 **shopping mall** (Am) shopping centre, indoor space with lots of shops

store, waving enthusiastically. "Ugh. I'm *obsessed* with these sunglasses!" she cried, pointing at them through the window. "A little on the expensive side, though," she admitted, indicating the four hundred dollar price tag. "But *you only live once*, right?"

Silvia was in her early twenties. She had long blonde hair and bright blue eyes. Right away, Detective Jacobs noticed her striking emerald necklace. "Yes, they are really nice sunglasses," she agreed, "but I'm on a budget. I bought mine online for twenty-five dollars," she added, adjusting them on her face. Silvia looked at her with pity.

"Oh, that's *so* sad," she moaned, sticking out her lower lip. "Well, I'm still in the *fun* stage of life–and I hope I never leave it!" she exclaimed, laughing at her own joke. The detective didn't know a lot about fashion. But she knew enough to estimate the cost of Silvia's high-end outfit: jeans, blouse, jacket, boots, designer bag–and emerald necklace. She was probably wearing thousands of dollars in clothes and accessories, not including the sunglasses she bought later. It was a fortune for a cashier in a museum gift shop.

"*Apparently, she can keep food on her table,*" thought Detective Jacobs with interest. Then, together, they walked in the direction of a frozen yogurt shop. "Can we stop here for a moment and talk?" she asked.

"Sure!" replied Silvia. She went inside at once and ordered a large swirl of strawberry in a cup. Then she waited for Detective Jacobs to pay for it.

"The disappearance of the pharaoh is such a puzzle," said the detective. "What are your thoughts?" Silvia slowly pulled the plastic spoon out of her mouth.

"My thoughts? Well, I'd *never* do a thing like that, Detective!" swore Silvia, placing a hand over her heart. "Can you imagine me

---

1 **to wave** to move your hand from side to side to greet sb or call their attention –
6 **striking** impressive – 11 **to moan** to say sth with an unhappy voice – 27 **puzzle** sth difficult to understand – 31 **to swear** to promise that you are telling the truth

in a jail cell? Wearing an *orange* jumpsuit every day? Ugh! And Sanjay is innocent too. He's really sweet. Felix, our custodian, is a decent man, so not him. Pierre is a bit pretentious–and thinks he knows everything about art. But he would not enjoy prison at all! Mrs. Harwood is far too old–and forgetful–to be a criminal. And I don't think it was either Charlotte or Amir. Selling the pharaoh, I suppose, would set them up for life. But they just got married– so why would they take a risk like that? That would be...crazy."

> Why did the detective go to the shopping center?

> What was surprising about Silvia?

Think about it...

> Why do you think it is important for some people to wear very expensive clothes?

> In choosing clothes to wear, what is important to you?

---

1 **jumpsuit** a piece of clothing that covers the upper and lower part of the body –
3 **pretentious** trying to appear smarter as a way to impress others – 7 **to set sb up** *(here)* to give sb money that will last a long time

---

Chapter 6

Detective Jacobs knew that art theft was one of the most high-profit, illegal activities in the world. Also called "trafficking in cultural property," it meant stealing things–like artifacts, sculptures, and paintings–from various locations: museums, private homes, galleries, places of worship, and archeological sites. The FBI and the EU's Interpol had pictures and descriptions of missing items in databases, but very little was ever recovered–generally less than ten percent.

The pharaoh was an ideal target, and it was not difficult to steal. Perhaps a wealthy buyer already had it. Or perhaps it needed to pass through a larger crime network, using smugglers and money-launderers, to make finding it nearly impossible. Ultimately, the pharaoh would end up with one billionaire or another, someone with an interest in collecting art, stolen or not.

Detective Jacobs had a lot to think about. Last night, she confirmed that Charlotte and Amir were legally married, an

---

18 **to traffic** (here) to sell things illegally – 21 **place of worship** building or space for religious practices – 23 **to recover** (here) to get back – 26 **smuggler** sb who moves things illegally from one place to another

interesting fact that neither of them had disclosed earlier. Today, however, she had to track down Pierre. He lived in a tiny bungalow in the woods, and it wasn't an easy place to find. It was a surprising environment for someone so cultured. "Welcome, Detective!" said Pierre in a strong French accent.

"I'll bet you don't get a lot of visitors out here," she remarked, exiting her car. "You aren't easy to find."

"I love the solitude," explained Pierre. "And it's such a contrast from my apartment in Paris." Pierre, a man in his mid-forties was dressed impeccably, looking a bit like a fish out of water.

"I went to Paris once," said Detective Jacobs. "What an incredible city! In which part did you live?"

"I live–I mean *lived*–near the Louvre Museum," he indicated. "I was actually a tour guide there for many years. Did you see it?"

"Well, I went for a short visit," admitted the detective. "I mean, a person could explore the Louvre for weeks–months–and not see it all. It was amazing." Detective Jacobs couldn't help but smile. "And yet, *now*, you work at the Westbrook Museum–and live, um, in the middle of nowhere." Pierre looked down on the ground and shook some dirt off his expensive shoes.

"I see beauty in all kinds of art," he responded, sniffing audibly. "People can appreciate works other than the *Mona Lisa* and the *Venus de Milo*. Believe me, the Westbrook has its charms–and so does my current habitat."

"Oh, yes, it definitely does," Detective Jacobs agreed, hearing no sound other than the wind in the trees. "Still, you must have been excited by the loan of the pharaoh. It was kind of a big deal for the Westbrook, wasn't it?"

"Well, of course, Detective," answered Pierre, rubbing his hands together nervously. "But the Louvre has a superb collection of

---

1 **to disclose** to reveal an unknown fact – 3 **bungalow** a house on one floor – 6 **to remark** to say sth – 8 **solitude** being alone – 10 **impeccably** perfectly – 22 **to sniff** to take air in through your nose

Egyptian artifacts. And I've seen much more impressive pieces than the one that was...sadly...lost."

"Well, sadly *stolen*," clarified Detective Jacobs. "And valued at over five million dollars." Pierre waved his hands in disgust.

"Pooh!" he exclaimed. "It's vulgar to give art a dollar amount, isn't it? But let me tell you what you really want to know: I didn't take the pharaoh. Yes, I was at the museum that night. But, like almost everyone else, I was–and still am–completely in the dark."

Which two characters did the detective discover were legally married?

What was Pierre's job at the Louvre Museum?

Think about it...

Why do you think Amir and Charlotte hid the fact that they were married?

Why do you think someone who is used to living in Paris would want to live in a small house in the middle of the woods?

5 **to exclaim** to say sth with emotion – 5 **vulgar** tasteless, unsophisticated

Chapter 7

Detective Jacobs hadn't eliminated any suspects yet. And, frankly, many of their behaviors concerned her. Sanjay nearly had a panic attack yesterday when she approached him after school. This time, the detective had to remind *him* to take a deep breath and let it out slowly. He was very young–only a junior in high school– but why would an innocent person react this way?

Charlotte and Amir were also on the detective's mind. Both of them were in positions of power; perhaps they were partners in life–and in crime–and needed the money to start new lives elsewhere. Amir was clearly in the process of moving, and five million dollars would surely be useful.

And how on Earth could Silvia afford her shopping habit? The *fun stage of life* required a lot of money, and where exactly was she getting it? Pierre, too, was a contradiction. Why was a sophisticated Parisian working at the Westbrook and living in the woods? It made no sense. And Mrs. Harwood? Detective Jacobs scratched her head. The executive director–*the richest woman around*–was very quick to blame others, and something just wasn't right with her story.

The next day, Detective Jacobs parked next to the Westbrook Museum. She'd actually looked forward to another conversation with Felix, the custodian, a man in his fifties. As promised, he was waiting for her at the entrance. He also observed that she was carrying his large, circular key ring, something that he'd surrendered to law enforcement officers after the robbery. "Ah, my keys!" he said, reaching toward the detective excitedly. "I've missed them!"

"Sorry," replied the detective, gripping the ring tightly. "They're still *my* keys for now. I went through them with Mrs. Harwood, matching each one with locks on doors, drawers, cabinets, and enclosures. However, two keys on this ring remain a mystery.

---

2 **to concern** to worry – 15 **sophisticated** sb who has a lot of knowledge of culture and fashion – 16 **woods** forest – 18 **to blame** to say sb is guilty of sth – 25 **to surrender** *(here)* to have to give up – 28 **to grip** to hold sth tightly

Detective Jacobs flipped up two long silver keys. "Do you have any idea what these are for?"

"Hmm," Felix answered, shrugging his shoulders. "They were probably from some display cases that we don't use anymore." Then Felix went inside with Detective Jacobs. Together, they walked down the stairs to the basement. Once again, they checked the fuse box. "So," said Felix, "as I've told you several times, someone came down here and cut off the power."

"And what about the backup generator?" inquired the detective.

"Well," responded Felix, adjusting a few strands of his thinning, gray hair, "the old thing hadn't worked in years. Mrs. Harwood claimed that a repair wasn't in the budget. I guess she learned that lesson the hard way."

"Felix," asked Detective Jacobs, "why weren't you carrying a flashlight when the lights went out? Wouldn't a custodian have one–or wear it on a utility belt–especially when he is about to handle something worth five million dollars?"

"Don't look at me!" Felix barked, his friendly expression disappearing. "I'll admit that mistakes were made," he continued, baring his coffee-stained teeth. "But, unlike the *real* thief, I didn't see that Egyptian artifact as a big payday. What would I do with it? To me, it was an old rock with a face on it. Too bad it's gone," he said, looking at the key ring in Detective Jacob's hand irritably. "But...easy come, easy go."

---

3 **to shrug** to move your shoulders up and down – 6 **basement** room in a building that is below the ground – 11 **strand** a single piece of hair – 19 **to bark** to make a loud noise – 21 **coffee-stained** when coffee changes the color of sth

Why was Felix excited to see Detective Jacobs?

After the power had been cut off, why didn't the backup generator work?

Think about it...

Why do you think Felix didn't see the Egyptian sculpture as a big payday?

Felix describes the pharaoh as "an old rock with a face on it". Yet, others see it as a priceless artifact. What do you think?

Chapter 8

Some people–like Felix, perhaps–naively supposed that art theft was a crime without victims. It didn't really matter that there was a market for old stuff, and a missing pharaoh was not the end of the world. Detective Jacobs, however, knew better. In many cases, stolen treasures were used for money–laundering, the process of making *dirty* money–earned through criminal activity–appear *clean*–or legal. She also realized that valuable artwork was sometimes collateral for loans in the underworld, financing drugs, weapons, and terrorism. "It's far more serious than losing *an old rock with a face on it*," she thought, driving up the steep road toward Cedar Hills, the exclusive area where Mrs. Harwood lived.

Detective Jacobs showed her badge to the security guard stationed at the gate to Mrs. Harwood's large estate. He looked

---

20 **victim** sb hurt by a crime or accident – 26 **collateral** sth given to make sure a loan is repaid – 26 **underworld** place for criminals and organized crime – 31 **to be stationed** to work at a particular place

---

like the same man who was her chauffeur. Then she parked outside an old, French-style chateau that was badly in need of repair. She was surprised to see Mrs. Harwood answer the door. At 11:30 a.m., it looked like the elderly woman had just gotten up. She was a bit disheveled, dressed in an old bathrobe and slippers. "I hope I'm not intruding," the detective said apologetically.

"Well, you are," sighed Mrs. Harwood with annoyance. "But you've come all this way, so come in. Have you figured out who stole the pharaoh? It was Sanjay, wasn't it? Or Charlotte...I told you that she was an opportunist."

"Not yet," answered Detective Jacobs, noting the interior of Mrs. Harwood's mansion. It was impressive–and probably spectacular once upon a time. But it was neglected now. There were sheets thrown over much of the furniture; the marble floors were chipped and the Persian rugs were threadbare and dusty. "You have a lovely home," said the detective, as they walked into a large room.

"Huh," Mrs. Harwood muttered, not really believing the compliment. "Well, houses get old...just like people. It's a lot to keep up a place like this," she declared. "Anyway, I doubt you came for the tour. What do you want?"

"The night of the robbery, you were at the Westbrook with your staff," stated Detective Jacobs. "Once again, exactly where was everyone and what was each person doing?"

"Detective," protested Mrs. Harwood, "I'm seventy-six years old. I can barely remember an hour ago. Who knows? Ask *them*!" As Mrs. Harwood spoke, Detective Jacobs quickly scanned the collection of art on her walls, some of it certainly valuable. Although she was no expert, one piece looked like a Rembrandt; another looked like a Picasso, a painting far more remarkable

2 **chateau** a large house in France – 5 **disheveled** very messy looking – 6 **to intrude** to come in uninvited – 8 **to figure sth out** to find the solution to a problem – 13 **once upon a time** a long time ago – 13 **to neglect** to not take care of – 15 **chipped** with small pieces broken – 15 **threadbare** worn through – 25 **to protest** to say sth in disagreement

than the pencil sketch in the Westbrook. Yet, it was clear that several paintings were missing. Where something had once hung, there was now a rectangular blank spot, highlighted by paint that was a darker color than the faded areas around it.

Detective Jacob's eyes continued to move around the room. Then she zeroed in on a modern portrait: a woman with long blonde hair and bright blue eyes, wearing a striking emerald necklace. It looked just like Silvia, the cashier in the museum gift shop! At that moment, Mrs. Harwood tugged on the detective's arm and hurriedly led her to the front door. "I have other things to do today," she said sternly. "I'm afraid that you'll have to go."

What was interesting about Mrs. Harwood's chateau?

What did the detective notice about the paintings on Mrs. Harwood's walls?

Think about it...

Valuable artwork is sometimes used as collateral for loans in the underworld. It can finance criminal activities such as narcotics, weapons, and terrorism. What do you think can be done to stop the theft of artwork?

1 **sketch** a quick drawing – 4 **faded** less bright in color than in the past – 6 **to zero in on** to focus your attention on sth – 11 **sternly** in a serious way

Chapter 9

As she left Cedar Hills, Detective Jacobs had a lot to think about.
More and more, she suspected Mrs. Harwood's involvement in
the robbery. The museum's executive director had the appearance
of being rich, but perhaps she had run out of cash. Her estate was
in poor condition, and she obviously didn't have the money to
maintain it.

The detective recalled the empty spaces on Mrs. Harwood's
walls. Was she selling off her own art collection? Also, what
would she gain by stealing the pharaoh? Surely, there was a big
insurance settlement–and a larger payout once the money was
laundered. Even so, she couldn't have committed this crime
alone. Was it possible that she and Silvia were related–and, more
importantly, were they accomplices?

Later that day, Detective Jacobs decided to talk to Charlotte
once again. When she arrived at her apartment, Amir opened the

---

18 **to suspect** to think that sb did sth – 20 **to run out of sth** to use all of sth – 20 **estate**
everything that sb owns when they die – 24 **to sell off** to sell sth at a lower price than
normal – 29 **accomplice** partner in crime

door. "So, this is where you've moved!" she observed cheerfully. "I suppose that makes sense."

"Hey, Detective," said Amir, holding a cup of red hibiscus tea. "You really like to surprise people, don't you?"

"Hello," Charlotte said, appearing at his side. "Please come in." Detective Jacobs entered the apartment and immediately noticed a large photo on the living room wall. It showed the Great Sphinx of Giza with the Pyramid of Khafre in the background.

"What an incredible picture!" exclaimed the detective, pointing enthusiastically at the image.

"It is, indeed," replied Amir, offering Detective Jacobs a chair. "And, so far, the Sphinx and the pyramids remain in Egypt. Too heavy to steal, I guess."

"Yes, fortunately," agreed the detective, nodding her head. "But on a different topic, I came here today to congratulate you. You're married! It's funny that you didn't tell me earlier."

"Thanks," uttered Charlotte quietly, her face turning red. "You see, we're very private people. There has been so much going on with the investigation. It just didn't seem...uh...*relevant*."

"Well, it could be *relevant*," responded Detective Jacobs, raising her eyebrows a little. "Secondly, Amir, I keep remembering our conversation about the theft of Egyptian artifacts–and their sale to collectors and museums."

"I meant everything I told you before. It's an *atrocity*!" he shouted. "Depriving Egyptians of a connection to their cultural beginnings is...in my opinion...a crime against humanity!"

"Amir," said Charlotte, as he sat down next to her on the sofa, "it disgusts me, too, when private collectors make art *invisible* to the rest of the world. However, I've worked in museums for many years," she continued. "In my experience–before the Westbrook– art was respectfully handled and shared with the public."

---

1 **cheerfully** in a happy way – 9 **to exclaim** to say sth enthusiastically – 17 **to utter** to say – 20 **relevant** connected to what is being investigated – 21 **eyebrow** the line of hair above the eyes – 24 **atrocity** a cruel and violent act – 28 **disgust** dislike sth very much

"And would it be fair," asked the detective, "for the Metropolitan Museum of Art, the Louvre, and the British Museum, for instance, to return the Egyptian artifacts that they've had for... in some cases...hundreds of years?"

"Well," answered Charlotte, "I don't really think that..."

"Artifacts belong to the culture that created them," interrupted Amir, standing up again abruptly. "So, yes! It would be fair!" Then he angrily set down his tea. "Detective, did you know that ninety percent of Africa's cultural heritage is located in the West? Does that sound *fair* to you? Yes, I had a good reason to take the pharaoh: returning it to Egypt where it rightfully belongs!"

"I'm not accusing you of taking anything," stated Detective Jacobs calmly.

"Yet," grumbled Amir, "you suspect me–or us–or you wouldn't be here right now. I'm sorry to say that the pharaoh is not back in Egypt. Instead, it's in the hands of some *despicable*, black market art dealer...but I didn't put it there!"

Why did the detective suspect that Mrs. Harwood was involved in the robbery?

Why didn't Charlotte and Amir tell the detective that they were married?

Think about it...

Do you think it's fair that museums display art that was originally stolen?

7 **abruptly** suddenly and unpleasantly – 16 **despicable** hateful

Chapter 10

Amir was very opinionated. But Detective Jacobs didn't think he was a liar. And even though Charlotte hadn't mentioned their marital status before, she seemed to be telling the truth. Yet, officially, they were still suspects, along with Mrs. Harwood, Silvia, Pierre, Felix, and Sanjay. As a result, the detective stayed in constant contact with them all, arranging meetings or visiting their homes unannounced.

It was 5:00 p.m. when Detective Jacobs finally returned to the police station. Inside her office, she stood in front of a large bulletin board that displayed photos, maps, and notes pertaining to the robbery. She looked at it intently, following the web of strings that connected people, places, and things. For example, there was a string between Mrs. Harwood and the ancient pharaoh. Unfortunately, she had little information beyond that.

Mrs. Harwood never really explained how the pharaoh came, momentarily, to the Westbrook. At first, she'd said it was a deal

---

16 **opinionated** sb who has very strong opinions about many things – 17 **liar** sb who tells lies – 18 **marital status** the state that defines if sb is married or not married – 22 **unannounced** without warning

with a private collector. Yet, she refused to provide more details: "He prefers to be anonymous." Then her story changed: "The pharaoh was owned by a large corporation. Hard to say why I was the lucky–or unlucky–one to borrow it." Later, she acted forgetful: "I don't actually recall who owned it. It passed through a chain of people in Europe. The art world has its secrets. Um, what was I saying?"

As expected, there were no records about something that was undoubtedly looted from Egypt long ago. The pharaoh didn't appear in any catalogs or databases. Before the robbery, neither the FBI nor Interpol had listed it as stolen. In the past, Egyptologists and art appraisers had believed it was authentic. So, it had probably been underground–illegally bought, sold or passed down–for many generations.

Perhaps Mrs. Harwood had kept the pharaoh for years, something to sell when she needed the money. Her personal history was hazy. She had a late husband, some kind of businessman. Apparently, they shared an interest in art. Mrs. Harwood played the role of a philanthropist. And in an effort to bring *art and culture to the people*, she established the Westbrook, a "third-rate collection," according to Charlotte, worth far less than anything in her home.

Detective Jacobs pinned another string between photos of Mrs. Harwood and Silvia. An advanced background check had revealed that Silvia was indeed her granddaughter. "A big payday would definitely cover fresh paint, improved flooring, and a new bathrobe for Mrs. Harwood," thought the detective, smiling. "She could hire a chauffeur *and* a security guard–and maybe a housekeeper or two. Silvia, meanwhile, could go to the mall seven days a week."

---

4 **to borrow** to take sth with the intention of returning it – 5 **to recall** to remember sth – 9 **undoubtedly** without a doubt – 12 **appraiser** expert who can tell how much sth is worth – 17 **hazy** not very clear – 17 **late** *(here)* dead – 19 **philanthropist** a rich person who helps the poor by giving money

The detective decided that now was the time for another conversation with Silvia. This thought, however, was interrupted by a knock on her office door. It was Sanjay, accompanied by his father. The boy was distraught and his father looked very worried. "Sanjay has something to tell you, Detective," said his father, putting a protective arm around his son. "Go ahead." Sanjay was extremely emotional and needed more than a few deep breaths before he could speak.

"It's okay," added Detective Jacobs reassuringly. "Sit down and take your time."

"He... told me that he would hurt me," cried Sanjay, dropping into a chair. "And...and...he said that he would...hurt my family," he continued, barely able to finish his sentence.

"Who said that to you, Sanjay?" exclaimed the detective. "Please give me his name!"

> Why did the detective want to speak to Silvia again?

> Why did Sanjay come with his father?

Think about it...

Who do you think threatened Sanjay?

---

4 **distraught** very upset – 9 **reassuringly** in a way that makes sb feel less worried

Chapter 11

"It was Fe...Fe...Felix," Sanjay sobbed, "the custodian. Lately, he's been following me everywhere," he added, his whole body trembling with fear. "He probably knows I'm here."

"Thank you for coming forward," Detective Jacobs said sincerely. "Believe me. He won't hurt you or anyone in your family. You'll have security around the clock. Can you please tell me what you saw–or felt–on the night of the robbery?" she asked, offering Sanjay a bottle of water.

"So, just before we lost power," he began nervously, "Felix told me to get a cloth and a spray bottle from the other side of the room. We needed to clean the glass before we locked up the pharaoh," he explained. "Then the lights went out. It was pitch-black–no one could see a thing!"

Sanjay described trying to feel his way back to the pharaoh, but someone pushed him hard in another direction. He knew it was Felix by the smell of his "awful coffee breath." Then he sensed that Felix had left the room. "He had to be wearing night-vision goggles or something, because he knew where he was going," Sanjay claimed. "Anyway, he'd returned by the time Silvia, Amir, and Charlotte found phones and flashlights to illuminate the area. Felix was flushed, though. He looked like he'd been running."

"Interesting," commented the detective. "What happened next?"

"The pharaoh was missing and everyone was in a panic. Mrs. Harwood and Pierre were yelling from another room–probably her office. The rest of us were scrambling around in the semi-darkness, looking for the pharaoh. Later, Felix–little wonder–found a flashlight too. Then he ran down to the basement and restored the power, looking like a big hero. Nevertheless, he knew...that I knew...that he'd shoved me, nearly knocking me down. So, before the police arrived, he took me aside and

3 **to tremble** to shake – 4 **to come forward** to volunteer to speak – 12 **pitch-black** extremely dark – 18 **goggles** special glasses that protect your eyes – 21 **flushed** red in the face – 26 **to scramble around** to run in a disorganized way – 29 **to restore** to bring sth back to normal – 30 **to shove** to push sb with strength

whispered: 'Not a word about this, Kid. Some things are none of your business.'"

"Do you have any idea where he put the pharaoh?" the detective inquired.

"Well," replied Sanjay, finally breathing more normally, "I've seen a safe behind a wall in Mrs. Harwood's office. There are several boxes in there too. The opening is hidden under a large, heavy tapestry. Two weeks ago, I went into her office to deliver the mail. She and Felix were standing in that back area, peering into the safe. They didn't notice me, though."

"Did you speak to them?" she asked.

"No," answered Sanjay honestly. "I left quickly. You know, none of my business."

Instantly, the detective assigned 24-hour protection to Sanjay and his family. Then she sent two police officers to Felix's home. Following Sanjay's statement, they needed to bring him in right away for questioning. Now, there was a strong case against both Felix and Mrs. Harwood. Hopefully, they would cooperate with law enforcement and expose everyone involved, locally and in the criminal underworld.

Detective Jacobs left immediately for the Westbrook, along with two additional policemen. However, she received a disappointing call just as they arrived. It was from one of the officers sent to pick up Felix. "Sorry to say that he isn't here," he reported.

"Well, wait until he returns home," the detective advised, sighing with exasperation. "Felix is dangerous and we absolutely have to detain him. Stay there all night if necessary."

"No, he *really* isn't here," clarified the officer. "His place is abandoned. The guy took off."

---

8 **tapestry** a piece of cloth with a picture on it – 16 **right away** immediately – 30 **to take off** to leave

How did Sanjay know it was Felix who pushed him?

Why did the detective assign 24-hour protection to Sanjay?

Think about it...

Why do you think Sanjay went to the police? Would you go to the police if you were being threatened?

Chapter 12

With Felix's keys in her hand, Detective Jacobs and two police officers ran up the museum steps, unlocked the building, and headed straight for Mrs. Harwood's office. The detective pulled aside the tapestry, revealing two locks on the wall. As expected, the mysterious, long silver keys instantly opened a secret door, exposing a small, temperature-controlled room containing a safe and several boxes. "How strange that Mrs. Harwood never took me to this area before," she said, a smile spreading across her face. "She forgot to show me the best part of the Westbrook." Detective Jacobs was surprised to see that the safe was unlocked– and empty. Yet, she was very intrigued by the boxes in the room. Could any of them contain the pharaoh? She opened one and then carefully cut through some layers of paper and plastic around a painting. "I studied art history in college," claimed one officer. "*That* looks like a *Da Vinci*!"

21 **to head** to go in a certain direction – 29 **intrigued** curious

"Why isn't it hanging in the Westbrook–for the public?" asked the other.

"This isn't about the museum business," the detective replied, gazing in disbelief at the fifteenth-century masterpiece. "It's about art trafficking, and I'm betting it was stolen." Immediately, she contacted the FBI art crimes division. "You won't believe what I've found hiding behind a wall at the Westbrook Museum," she informed an agent. "You must come now!"

Two hours later, three FBI agents and six additional police officers were on the scene. The agents had the expertise to handle priceless art, and they immediately began searching national and international databases. After examining the contents of nine boxes in the secret room, it was determined that every piece–valued for enormous amounts–had been stolen. "We're a little late for the pharaoh, I guess," sighed Detective Jacobs, shaking her head. "Apparently, they were in a bigger hurry to move that one." Meanwhile, other officers had been sent up to Cedar Hills to arrest Mrs. Harwood, but no one was there.

Earlier that day, Mrs. Harwood knew that she was in trouble. And she was upset after Detective Jacobs left her home. Mrs. Harwood didn't imagine that the detective could identify priceless pieces of art. After all, they surely didn't teach such things at the police academy. But she certainly noticed the portrait of Silvia. Immediately, she got on the phone and called Felix. "That annoying detective is connecting the dots," she hissed. "Meet me at the Westbrook–back stairs–in an hour," she commanded. "We have to move now."

Felix was more than ready to move. In fact, he'd already rented a moving truck to get out of town. They couldn't leave without the pharaoh, though. So, while Detective Jacobs was meeting with Charlotte and Amir, Felix and Mrs. Harwood were breaking into

---

4 **disbelief** not being able to believe what you can see – 10 **scene** the place where a crime has been commited – 10 **expertise** skill to do a particular job – 24 **portrait** a painting of sb – 25 **to connect the dots** to use pieces of information to understand sth – 26 **to hiss** to make a sound of disapproval – 31 **to break into** to enter a place illegally

the Westbrook. It was easy enough because Mrs. Harwood had her own keys and the security–as Amir had said–was appalling. Within minutes, they opened the safe in the secret room and put the pharaoh into an empty ice chest. The rest of the treasures had to stay hidden a while longer.

It was after midnight by the time the FBI had seized everything else in the Westbrook's secret room. Although Detective Jacobs was exhausted, she knew that her work wasn't finished. "Hopefully, we're not too late," she said to a group of officers. "But, uh, there's a man from France living in a tiny bungalow in the woods. We have to check on him. And it really can't wait."

What did the silver keys open?

What did the detective find in the boxes?

Think about it...

Why weren't the paintings in the secret room displayed at the Westbrook Museum?

2 **appalling** very bad – 4 **ice chest** a large box to keep sth cold – 6 **to seize** to take back items that have been stolen

Chapter 13

Detective Jacobs had never believed Pierre's story. She didn't buy his fake humility or that he could *see beauty in all kinds of art*, at the Louvre or at the Westbrook. More than solitude, he needed a hiding place for people–or things. And while it was *vulgar to give art a dollar amount*, Pierre was quite possibly getting rich from its black-market price tag. Also, a tour guide definitely didn't earn enough to live near the Louvre. A successful art trafficker, on the other hand, could comfortably live there with a nice view of the Seine.

Pierre had no employment record at the Louvre. Of course, he might have worked under many names–real or assumed–depending on the character he played. Without question, though, he had ties to Mrs. Harwood, beyond his phony job at the Westbrook. The detective suspected that Pierre was her

---

31 **ties** things that connect sb to another person – 31 **phony** fake

go-between. He moved art from her hands and then delivered it–directly or indirectly–to a buyer, taking a percentage of the profits.

Detective Jacobs had to find Pierre immediately. She and several officers sped as fast as they could to his location in the woods. She was surprised to see a moving truck parked there, partially hidden in the trees. Luckily, however, his bungalow was still occupied. There was a dim light on inside, and she heard the familiar voices of three individuals: Mrs. Harwood, Felix, and Pierre.

Without a knock or an invitation, the officers barged inside. "Hands up!" Detective Jacobs shouted. "You're all under arrest!" The look of shock on their faces was something the detective would never forget. Dressed in dark clothes and carrying large amounts of cash, they were clearly preparing to go somewhere. "It looks like you're getting ready to leave this charming place," she observed. "Sorry that you'll have to postpone your departure for a while."

"You've made a terrible mistake, Detective!" cried Mrs. Harwood, clutching her heart for dramatic effect. "These men… they're…they're blackmailing me! They have the precious Egyptian pharaoh, and I'll show you where it's hidden."

"Enough, *Madame*," ordered Pierre. "Mrs. Harwood organized the whole thing–the guiltiest one of all. And she's been in the art theft game for many years. We just got trapped in her web, right Felix?" Felix wasn't listening. Instinctively, he tried to run away, but a group of officers stopped his attempt and handcuffed him to a chair.

"There's no need to *show* me where the pharaoh is hidden, Mrs. Harwood," said the Detective Jacobs, ignoring the scuffle. "Let me

8 **dim** weak – 16 **charming** beautiful and pleasant – 20 **to clutch** to hold sth tightly –
21 **to blackmail** to get money or force sb to do sth by threatening to reveal a secret –
27 **to handcuff** *(here)* to lock sb to sth using metal rings around their wrists – 30 **scuffle** a
small fight involving a few people

guess where it is. Uh, is it in this ice chest?" she asked, pointing
to it on the floor. "Or are these just some snacks for your road
trip?" Carefully, the detective opened the ice chest. And there it
was–the missing pharaoh, an artifact far more striking than it had
appeared in photos. In fact, the sight of it took Detective Jacob's
breath away. Then she looked at Felix, still struggling in the chair.
"I must say, Felix, you've gone to a lot of trouble to steal *an old
rock with a face on it.*"

"It was Mrs. Harwood's idea," he complained angrily. "She..."

"You have the right to remain silent," Detective Jacobs read
aloud. "Anything you say can and will be used against you in a
court of law..."

> Whose house was going to
> be used as a hiding place?

> Who tried to run away
> when the police were
> trying to arrest them?

Think about it...

> What do you think was wrong with Mrs. Harwood's
> plan?

4 **striking** impressive

Chapter 14

Mrs. Harwood, Felix, and Pierre faced a variety of criminal charges relating to cultural property: theft, fraud, looting, and trafficking across state and international lines, to name a few. Although Felix and Pierre were sent to prison, their sentences were lighter than Mrs. Harwood's. She faced multiple counts of every charge and would likely spend the rest of her life incarcerated. Her estate and assets–mostly stolen art–were seized and the Westbrook was closed permanently.

In her discussions with Detective Jacobs and the FBI, Mrs. Harwood admitted to organizing the scheme with the pharaoh. "Initially, I'd decided to display it in the Westbrook for a few weeks. I thought I'd give, you know, *the people* a real treat– something to brighten their lives," she explained. "But it seemed

---

19 **to face** to accept sth that you have to deal with – 20 **fraud** getting money by cheating people – 25 **incarcerated** in prison – 28 **scheme** a plan that involves doing sth dishonest

more sensible to get that big insurance settlement and then sell it. And, yes, I formed the corporation that owned it and demanded that it be insured," she added. "I desperately needed the cash, and the Westbrook already had the Picasso sketch that used to hang in my bathroom."

Mrs. Harwood had planned to move to Switzerland, spending her retirement in "a nice chalet" in the countryside. "Naturally, that required money," she said, sighing. "Bit by bit, I was selling off my art collection. Pierre was helping me with that, of course. He also cut off the power the night of the robbery. Felix helped too–for a significant price–yet the man is a complete oaf."

Mrs. Harwood intended to seal up the old house and never return. When she died, she'd leave what was left to Silvia–and she could deal with "all of the legal issues." Silvia could also run the museum, she supposed. "My granddaughter was not involved in art trafficking, though. And, truth be told, she isn't smart enough to be a criminal."

Pierre also cooperated, to some extent, with the authorities. He actually provided a list of smugglers and buyers on the black market. And these people would be prosecuted too. Naturally, it was risky to give information about organized crime networks, and undoubtedly he would require a new name and address upon his release–but he was used to reinventing himself.

Silvia was very distressed by her grandmother's arrest. In spite of keeping their relationship a secret in the workplace, she and Mrs. Harwood had great affection for each other. Mrs. Harwood had even commissioned her granddaughter's portrait–the one item that Silvia was allowed to keep after her grandmother went to prison.

It broke Silvia's heart to see her grandmother in handcuffs– and realize that her bank account was now empty. "How will I

---

1 **settlement** an agreement that ends a problem – 8 **bit by bit** little by little – 11 **oaf** an unintelligent person – 20 **prosecuted** when someone is officially accused of having committed a crime – 24 **distressed** worried – 27 **to commission** to ask sb to do a special job, like painting a portrait

bear it, Detective Jacobs? My life will be so...different now. The
Westbrook is closed...and I'll...I'll have to get a *job*!"

"I think a lot of stores at the mall are hiring," she replied, trying to
be helpful. "Sorry, but the *fun stage of life* had to end sooner or later."

"And my poor grandmother might have to wear an orange
jumpsuit! How horrible!" she cried. "Deep down, she's a *good*
person–and it's so *unfair*!"

"What your grandmother did was *unfair*, Silvia," said Detective
Jacobs seriously. "Like it or not, she was part of an illegal crime
network that helped to finance drugs, weapons, and terrorism–not
to mention her involvement in the shameful looting of cultural
property. I've learned that art theft is a crime against humanity–and
it has many victims. I'm sorry, but there is nothing *good* about it."

How did Pierre
cooperate with the
authorities?

What was Mrs. Harwood's
plan after the theft?

Think about it...

Do you think Pierre should get a lighter sentence
for helping the police?

Chapter 15

One year later, the FBI was still sorting out Mrs. Harwood's complicated art collection. Some things were returned to museums or private owners, but where did they truly belong? Was a particular piece *legally* acquired? Or was it looted and then sold, according to the laws centuries ago? Whenever possible, though, the goal of both the FBI and Interpol was *repatriation*– returning items to their culture of origin.

Sanjay was now a senior in high school. Detective Jacobs awarded him an Outstanding Citizen award, and a local service organization recognized his bravery with a college scholarship. Although Sanjay was frightened by his experience at the Westbrook, he was also grateful for it. He now had a keen interest in art theft and its impact around the world. He even dreamed of a career in the FBI, hoping someday to identify and repatriate cultural property.

---

24 **repatriation** returning sth to its place of origin – 29 **frightened by** afraid of

Egypt wasn't the only nation determined to repossess their artifacts. There were also efforts in India, Greece, China, Italy, Peru, Nigeria, Cambodia, Iraq, Congo, and many other countries to reclaim theirs. Nevertheless, many of the world's greatest museums still displayed art that was–originally–stolen. Was this practice acceptable in the twenty-first century? There were some museums that readily returned controversial objects, but others refused to let go, citing permanent, binding contracts–albeit shady ones–from the distant past.

Meanwhile, Amir and Charlotte were living happily in New York. Amir got a much better job as a security officer and Charlotte landed a position with a prestigious art gallery, a welcome change and a higher salary. Soon after they moved to New York, Charlotte took Amir to the Metropolitan Museum's collection of ancient Egyptian art, a display of thousands of cultural artifacts. According to the website, most of it was collected from years of archaeological work over a century ago, "a response to increasing Western interest in the culture of ancient Egypt."

"Huh," said Amir crossly. "More like a response to increasing Western interest in *stealing* the culture of ancient Egypt." Charlotte, however, thought the collection was extraordinary and absolutely loved the Temple of Dendur.

"Isn't this incredible?" she asked, pulling her husband by the hand. "Amir, look! This temple was actually a *gift* from Egypt in the 1960s. And imagine the number of people–from all over the world–who can see it here."

"It's impressive," agreed Amir. "But it still isn't right."

"Well," sighed Charlotte, "perhaps it's not right in your opinion." Amir preferred to remember their honeymoon trip two months earlier. For the first time, he had visited Egypt, the land of his ancestors. A highlight was exploring the Museum of Egyptian

8 **to cite** to quote – 9 **shady** not very honest – 25 **temple** a building that is used for worship

Antiquities in Cairo. With a map of the museum in their hands, Amir and Charlotte went directly to the glass enclosure around *the pharaoh*–the very one that had passed through the Westbrook.

They recognized it immediately, gazing at its almond-shaped eyes, full lips, and serene expression, sculpted in stone. How incredible that it was over three thousand years old. "And here in Egypt once again," said Amir, brushing tears from his eyes.

"I'm so glad this piece, in particular, was repatriated," observed Charlotte. "Can you imagine an artifact like this collecting dust in Mrs. Harwood's basement–or hidden in a secret room? It's unthinkable!"

"Seeing it here actually restores my faith in humanity," stated Amir. "It's where it belongs, Charlotte. It's a matter of national pride. And when all is said and done, it is...in a word...*fair*."

Which awards did Sanjay receive for his bravery?

Where did Amir and Charlotte move?

Think about it... ?

How easy do you think it would be for museums to change their ethical approach to displaying stolen artwork?

5 **serene** peaceful

Activities

Focus on the story

1. Are the sentences True or False?
Tick the correct box.

		True	False
1.	An Egyptian pharaoh was stolen from the Westbrook Museum.	☐	☐
2.	A very expensive Picasso sketch was also stolen from the Westbrook Museum.	☐	☐
3.	A Picasso sketch is the most valuable thing the museum had on display.	☐	☐
4.	Mrs. Harwood was the museum's curator.	☐	☐
5.	Amir thought it was ethical to display Egyptian artifacts in museums around the world.	☐	☐
6.	Silvia was wearing a $25 pair of sunglasses.	☐	☐
7.	Art trafficking is one of the most profitable illegal activities in the world.	☐	☐
8.	Pierre lives in a very expensive flat in the city centre.	☐	☐
9.	Amir and Charlotte are married.	☐	☐
10.	Felix went to the detective's office to confess.	☐	☐
11.	There was a secret door in Mrs. Harwood's office.	☐	☐
12.	Felix had rented a moving truck.	☐	☐

2. In which order were the places mentioned?

Put the following places in the order they were mentioned in the book.

1 New York
2 the Louvre Museum
3 the Westbrook Museum
4 Pierre's bungalow
5 the shopping mall
6 Mrs. Harwood's Chateau
7 the museum's secret room
8 Amir's apartment

3. What happened where?

Match the place with the event that happened there.

1	the Westbrook Museum	a	The suspects were arrested here.
2	Mrs. Harwood's chateau	b	The place where the pharaoh was stolen.
3	Switzerland	c	The place where they found all the stolen art.
4	the hidden room in the museum	d	The place Detective Jacobs thought was run down.
5	Pierre's bungalow	e	The place where Mrs. Harwood wanted to escape.

Focus on the people

1. Who did what?

Read the sentences and decide which character above did what.

Detective Jacobs   Silvia   Amir x2   Charlotte Mrs. Harwood   Pierre   Sanjay x3

1 .... had a job with the FBI as well as her normal job.

2 .... didn't want to go to prison because of having to wear an orange jumpsuit.

3 .... didn't want to let Detective Jacobs into their home.

4 .... was a junior in high school.

5 .... thinks it's disgusting when private collectors make art invisible to the rest of the world.

6 .... wanted to move to Switzerland.

7 .... got a deal with the police.

8 .... got an outstanding citizen award.

9 .... wants to work for the FBI in the future.

10 .... is very happy to see pieces repatriated.

2. What do you know about them?

Write a profile for Mrs. Harwood and another character from the book. Compare them with your partner.

Name: Mrs. Harwood		Name: _____	
Interest: Residence: Important possession: Desired place of residence:		Interest: Residence: Important possession: Desired place of residence:	

Focus on grammar

1. Conditional sentences

Complete the conditional sentences by putting the verbs into the correct form.

1 If Detective Jacobs _____ (not study) art, she _____ (would not be) able to solve the case.

2 If Felix _____ (not drink) coffee, Sanjay _____ (would not be) able to identify him in the dark.

3 If Charlotte and Amir _____ (tell) people their secret, they _____ (might not be) suspects.

4 If Pierre _____ (not leave) Paris, he _____ (would not be) involved in this theft.

5 If Sanjay _____ (not come forward) with the truth, the detective _____ (might not be able) to solve the case.

2. Linking words

Fill in the gaps with one connector from the box.

although	however	so	because	but

1 Detective Jacobs knew one of them stole the pharaoh, _____ she didn't have enough evidence to prove it.

2 Sanjay was afraid of coming forward _____ he was threatened.

3 _____ Amir and Charlotte acted very suspiciously, they didn't commit any crimes.

4 Felix's breath was very strong, _____ it was easy to identify him.

5 Sanjay didn't want to confess, _____, his father forced him to.

Build your vocabulary

Focus on words

1. What's the word?

Unscramble the words so that they make up a word about crime and punishment. Write the correct word in the first column.

	loto	sth stolen during a violent event such as a riot
	tfeht	the act of stealing
	least	to take sth that belongs to sb else
	ialnmric	sb who commits a crime
	kblca tekarm	places where illegal things are sold
	rednurowdl	the world of criminals
	esucetorp	to start legal proceedings after sb has committed a crime
	rrstea	when the police take sb into custody
	liamkclab	to make sb pay you money because you know sth about them that they don't want other people to know

2. Phrasal verbs with *out*

Match the phrasal verb to the definition.

to let it out	to organize
to go out (electricity)	to force liquid out of your mouth
to find out	when the electricity stops working
to drive out	to discover
to spit out	to force sth or sb out of a place
to sort out	to make a loud sound

The Stolen Pharaoh – the mind map

Expand the mind map with words from the story and other words you know.

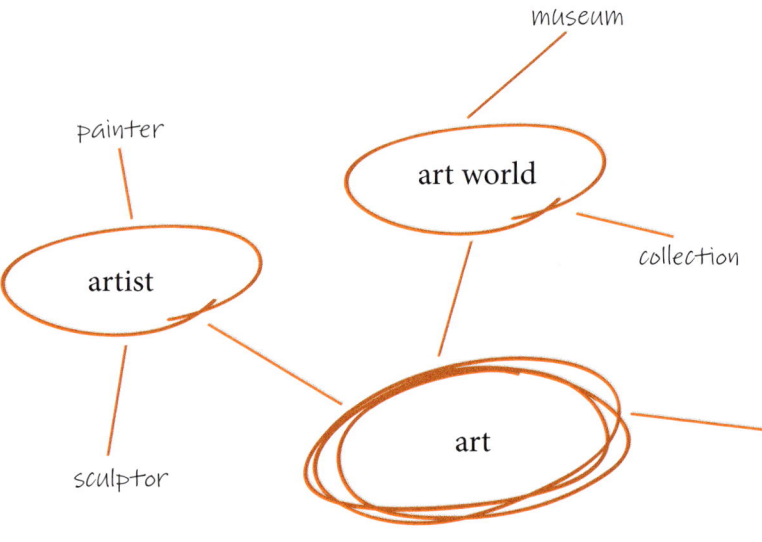

museum

painter

art world

collection

artist

art

sculptor

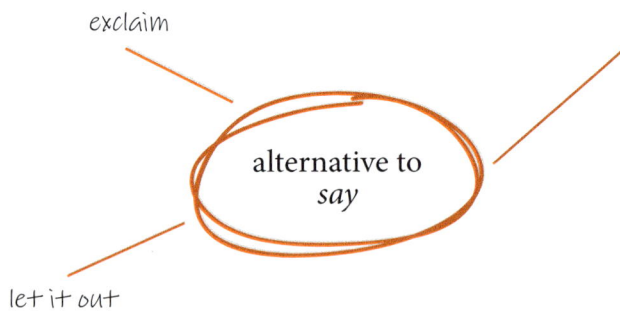

exclaim

alternative to *say*

let it out

crime

thief

steal

talking about crime

detective

The Stolen Pharaoh

law

arrest

housing

mansion

apartment

Glossary

	New word?	Notes / connected words

Art

antiquity	☐
appraiser	☐
artifact	☐
collection	☐
commission	☐
curator	☐
custodian	☐
display	☐
exhibition	☐
museum	☐
painter	☐
painting	☐
portrait	☐
private collector	☐
sculpt	☐
sculpture	☐
showcase	☐
sketch	☐
tapestry	☐
value	☐

Crime and punishment

blackmail	☐
black market	☐
break into	☐
commit a crime	☐
criminal	☐
dirty money	☐
go-between	☐
guilty	☐

	New word?	Notes / connected words
launder money	☐	
loot	☐	
robbery	☐	
smuggler	☐	
steal	☐	
terrorism	☐	
theft	☐	
trafficking	☐	
underground	☐	
underworld	☐	
victim	☐	

Law enforcement

	New word?	Notes / connected words
accuse	☐	
arrest	☐	
detective	☐	
handcuff	☐	
interrogate	☐	
prison	☐	
prosecute	☐	
recover	☐	
scene	☐	
seize	☐	
suspect	☐	

Housing

	New word?	Notes / connected words
apartment	☐	
basement	☐	
bungalow	☐	
chalet	☐	
chateau	☐	
estate	☐	
mansion	☐	

	New word?	Notes / connected words

Feelings

disgust	☐
distraught	☐
frightened	☐
happy	☐
scared	☐
upset	☐

Alternative to *say*

bark	☐
claim	☐
declare	☐
exclaim	☐
grumble	☐
hiss	☐
let it out	☐
moan	☐
scream	☐
state	☐
utter	☐
yell	☐

Find out more

Find out more

1. Art theft
Art theft is a very serious, yet common crime. Go online and find 10 interesting facts about how this crime affects society.

The impact of art theft on society

1.
2.
3.
4.
5.
6.
7.
8.
9.
10.

2. Famous art heists
There have been some very famous art heists. Go online, find an example and look for the information below.

- What was stolen
- How much it was worth
- When it was stolen
- How it was stolen
- Whether or not it has been recovered

Present your findings to your classmates.

Answer key

Focus on the story

Questions at the end of each chapter

Chapter 1
- An Egyptian Pharaoh
- Over 3000 years

Chapter 2
- Sanjay is young and kids often play silly pranks.
- She knows that any legitimate organization, such as a museum or auction house, would know it's stolen.

Chapter 3
- Master of Fine Arts
- She thinks that it's mediocre.

Chapter 4
- She worked in local law enforcement, and she was also assisting a part of the FBI that focused on art crimes.
- He resents that most of them were looted from his country.

Chapter 5
- She wanted to talk to Silvia, a young woman who worked at the gift shot.
- Silvia, a gift shop employee on a modest salary, was wearing very expensive clothes.

Chapter 6
- Charlotte and Amir are married.
- Pierre was a tour guide at the Louvre for many years.

Chapter 7
- He was excited because she had his keys.
- The backup generator had been broken for years.

Chapter 8
- The house was in need of repair.
- The paintings looked very valuable.

Chapter 9
- She considered her estate was in poor condition, and it looked like she needed money.
- They thought it wasn't relevant to the investigation.

Chapter 10
- She suspects Mrs. Harwood is her grandmother.
- He wanted to share some very important information with the detective. He wanted his father there for support.

Chapter 11
- He could smell Felix's breath, which stank of coffee.
- She wanted to protect Sanjay and his family because Felix had threatened them.

Chapter 12
- They opened a secret door exposing a safe and many boxes.
- She found a lot of expensive stolen paintings.

Chapter 13
- Pierre's house was going to be used as a hiding place.
- Felix tried to run away.

Chapter 14
- He gave them a list of smugglers and buyers on the blackmarket.
- She wanted to move to nice chalet in Switzerland.

Chapter 15
- He received an Outstanding Citzen award, and a local service organization gave him a college scholarship.
- They moved to New York.

Focus on the story

1 1 T, 2 F, 3 T, 4 F, 5 F, 6 F, 7 T, 8 F, 9 T, 10 F, 11 T, 12 T

2 The Westbrook Museum **Chapter 1**, The Louvre Museum
Chapter 1, New York **Chapter 2**, Amir's apartment **Chapter 4**,
the shopping mall **Chapter 5**, Mrs. Harwood's chateau
Chapter 8, Pierre's bungalow **Chapter 6**, the museum's secret
room **Chapter 12**

3

The Westbrook Museum	The place where the pharaoh was stolen.
Mrs. Harwood's chateau	The place Detective Jacobs thought was run down.
Switzerland	The place where Mrs. Harwood wanted to escape.
The hidden room in the museum	The place where they found all the stolen art.
Pierre's bungalow	The place where the suspects were arrested.

Focus on the people

1. 1 Detective Jacobs, 2 Silvia, 3 Amir, 4 Sanjay, 5 Charlotte,
   6 Mrs. Harwood, 7 Pierre, 8 Sanjay, 9 Sanjay, 10 Amir

2. Profile

Name: Mrs. Harwood	Name: _____
Interest: Art	Interest:
Residence: A large estate	Residence:
Important possession: portrait of Silvia	Important possession:
Desired place of residence: Switzerland	Desired place of residence:

Focus on grammar

1 Conditional sentences

  1 If Detective Jacobs hadn't studied art, she wouldn't have been able to solve the case.

  2 If Felix hadn't drunk coffee, Sanjay wouldn't have been able to identify him in the dark.

  3 If Charlotte and Amir had told people their secret, they might not have been suspects.

  4 If Pierre hadn't left Paris, he wouldn't have been involved in this theft.

  5 If Sanjay hadn't come forward with the truth, the detective might not have been able to solve the case.

2. Linking words

  1 Detective Jacobs knew one of them stole the pharaoh, but she didn't have enough evidence to prove it.

  2 Sanjay was afraid of coming forward because he was threatened.

  3 Although Amir and Charlotte acted very suspiciously, they didn't commit any crimes.

  4 Felix's breath was very strong, so it was easy to identify him.

  5 Sanjay didn't want to confess; however, his father forced him to.

Focus on words

1.

loot	loto	stolen during a violent event such as a riot
theft	tfeht	the act of stealing
steal	least	to take sth that belongs to sb else
criminal	ialnmric	sb who commits a crime
black market	kblca tekarm	places where illegal things are sold
underworld	rednurowdl	the world of criminals
prosecute	esucetorp	to start legal proceedings after sb has committed a crime
arrest	rrstea	when the police take sb into custody
blackmail	liamkclab	to make sb pay you money because you know sth about them that they don't want other people to know

2.

to let it out	to make a loud sound
to go out (electricity)	when the electricity is interrupted
to find out	to discover
to drive out	to force sth or sb out of a place
to spit out	to force liquid out of your mouth
to sort out	to organize